Victim in Pursuit (V.I.P.)
A Mother's Nightmare
My Life, My Story

Adina Hodge

Copyright © 2019 All rights reserved.

NO PART OF THIS PUBLICATION MAY BE REPRODUCED, STORED IN A RETRIEVAL SYSTEM, OR TRANSMITTED IN ANY FORM OR BY ANY MEANS, ELECTRONIC, MECHANICAL, PHOTOCOPY, RECORDING, OR ANY OTHER, WITHOUT THE PRIOR WRITTEN PERMISSION OF THE AUTHOR.

Edited by Latanya "Epiphany" Richardson

Dedication

To my loving sisters, thank you both for being my strength that helped me to get through this book. To my loving son, one day you will read this book, and understand why Mommy had to work so hard.

Special dedication to my forever loving Grandmother (and name sake); Adina L Hodge, may you forever rest in Heaven. Happy 100 Birthday 9-19-19. Love you Ma, this is for you.

To my family, I love you all and truly hope that this book is a blessing to everyone, I am no longer bound by my past. I am Free. I hope that you will all be free one day as well.

For all of the women who did not have a voice to say "No," and all young girls who were taken advantage of because they did not know any better, this is for you.

Table of Contents

Dedication 5

Preface 9

Chapter 1 15
(Victim in Pursuit) Begins...

Chapter 2 23
Professional by Day

Chapter 3 31
My Life Flashes Before My Eyes

Chapter 4 37
The Vicious Cycle

Chapter 5 41
A New Habit

Chapter 6 45
Turning to God

Chapter 7 51
Backsliding

Chapter 8 57
Self-Sabotage

Chapter 9 61
Life Continues

Chapter 10 65
God's Plan, Not Mine

Some of the Red Flags and Signs for Parents To look Out for! 69

Note from the Author 71

About the Author 72

Preface

This book is my coming out story. In it I talk about a lot of deep personal issues. I discuss somethings that are private. I talk about things that most women care not to disclose, in fear of what others may think about them. I'm not concerned about what others will think because I have overcome. I have conquered many of the issues that plagued me growing up and made it out of the statistical realm. (I'll come back to that later).

When you think about it, Life is always good until it takes a wrong turn for you or your loved ones. We may not have had a choice on how or whether we were brought into this world, nor could we control how we were raised. All we could and now can do is hope that our parents or guardians are people of integrity and morals. We hope that they want the very best for us. It sounds good, but that is not everyone's situation.

The Bible says, *"Train up a child in the way he should go: and when he is old, he will not depart from it,"* (Proverbs 22:8). I was raised by my maternal grandparents until the age of thirteen. Something happened when I turned thirteen and it felt as if my life fell apart.

My grandparents were my world, they were my everything. My maternal grandparents took custody of my siblings and I when we were young. You're probably wondering what happened to my mother and father right? Well the truth is nothing happened to them. In fact, they are still alive and are working on being the best version of themselves. My mother and father were caught up in the things of this world.

It wasn't always this way. They started off with a normal life. My mother and father were married, then they created me. They lived together for a short period of time before things became sour. They were both caught up in their own lives. Eventually, my grandmother, "May she forever Rest in Heaven" took on the responsibility of caring for my siblings and me.

My grandparents gave us the world. When I was thirteen, my grandparents passed away approximately a month apart from each other. My brother, sister and I were devastated. They were all we had. I didn't know or understand how to deal with their loss.

So, in turn I blamed myself. I was to blame...I took the guilt onto myself. I was a teenager, going through puberty and just starting out high school. I was young, dumb, and already becoming way too promiscuous. My young mind couldn't fathom, nor did I want to accept the fact that my world was over. Instead, I created a new world. My mother's sister took custody over my brother and I as well as my three-year-old baby sister. We moved into her house with her, and her adopted son at the time.

There was plenty of room at my aunt's house, minus the structure our grandparents provided us with. My aunt tried hard to fill in the void of our loss, but it just wasn't the same. At only thirteen, I did what I wanted and came and left, as I pleased. I totally ignored my Aunt's attempts at discipline. My brother was my only voice of reason. The only time I listened was when he got involved. As my older brother, I looked up to him. Besides, he had always protected me and my younger sister.

My first two years of high school were horrible. Towards the end of my high school year, still morning the loss of my grandparents, I decided to switch schools and go to an alternative high school. This move was catapulted by the fear that I would not be able to graduate on time. It didn't help that in the new school I started hanging out with the wrong crowd, staying out late, and drinking to mask my pain.

Who was there to show me or give me an example of what love should look like? The only source of love and stability I'd ever known were both gone. My grandparents were no longer around, my mom and father were caught up their own vices. I was looking for **Love**. Who was going to love me, was the question I kept asking myself?

During the 90's they had so many programs for teenagers that taught us about health education. They made it look and sound so exciting until most of us wanted to experiment with having sex. After all, they taught us what to do, how to go about it, and the proper way to protect oneself.

I was thirteen years old the night I decided to become a woman. I used so many excuses to convince myself that this was okay and something I was ready for. I wanted desperately to fit in with my peers and secretly felt like I would be in the "In" crowd once I crossed that bridge. Finally, I took that leap, and did it, with no regrets. At least so I thought.

My grandparents were able to see their 50th wedding anniversary before they parted. That lead me to believe that no matter what, when you find someone to love you never let that person go... When I got in a relationship with a man who told me he loved me, I believed him. Then I learned how easy it was for a guy to manipulate a young girl into getting her in the bedroom. Older guys took advantage of me. They spoiled me with things just to get me in bed and when they were tired, they left. I got tired of being hurt so I slowed down from being involved in these types of relationships. I focused on graduating from high school.

Living with my aunt was hard. She meant well but she was set in her ways. She truly relied on the money the government was giving her for us. I used to complain that I couldn't get much because my aunt did not have patience. She would take me to the department stores and tell me I had five minutes to get what I needed, while she was standing by the register. I never tried on anything. I would just grab what I thought would look good and bring it the counter. I felt so frustrated inside, because some of my clothing was either super tight or super big. To make matters worse I felt uncomfortable around her adoptive son. I was convinced he was mentally challenged. He would do weird things around the house I remember reporting that to the social worker who would show up once a month to see how things were going.

When I turned seventeen, I remember arguing with my aunt. She and I had a heated argument after her adoptive son, had trashed my room. I was tired of being in her household, watching her mismanage money, and being treated as if we were not her real family. So, we argued, she called the cops on me and kicked me out of her house, after witnessing me take photos of the damage her adoptive son had caused to my belongings.

During this time, (before my aunt kicked me out) my cousin who started modeling, invited me to one of her fashion shows. She suggested I become a model like her. She introduced me to the guy who helped her get started. She told me he was a talent scout, and fashion designer. I was excited about the opportunity and embarked upon a journey that what would change my entire life...

Chapter 1
(Victim in Pursuit) Begins...

I began modeling for the fashion designer. He told me to meet him at his studio in the city to try on clothing. I remember I went there the first day and I tried on several garments. Some of the clothes were very nice while the rest were way too sexy. He said, "I'm having an Adult fashion show. I need you too Model some lingerie. I was nervous but way too scared to say no. I figured if my cousin was doing it, then this could not possibly be that bad. As I was trying on the sexy clothing and lingerie, he poured some alcohol into a glass.

He said it was to make me feel a little more comfortable. I did not think anything of it. I drank until I had a buzz. He began showing me how he wanted me to walk in his garments. He moved closer and began fondling me. He groped and touched on my body while telling me how he wanted me to showcase his stuff. I stood frozen and uncomfortable. He became erect and then asked me to get a "bag." I was totally oblivious to what he was talking about or planning to do. He said, "Come over here and sit on my lap." That was when I realized that he was attempting to have sex with me. I nervously said, "No, thank you!" before running into the bathroom to change my clothes.

Reflect: We often get Red flags and ignore them. Why do we do that? Think about a time that you saw all the red flags and ignored them. Journal about the first signal, and what made you continue on with the decision that you knew would not be healthy for you. Release it and let it go, forgive yourself.

_____

_____

_____

_____

_____

_____

_____

_____

_____

_____

_____

_____

_____

I should have seen the red flags. Unfortunately, I wanted desperately to be accepted. So, instead of leaving that situation I decided to continue and do the showcase. I had so much fun modeling in the fashion show. It was fun but another part of me was extremely nervous.

Once the show was completed, he came up to me. He said, "Come on, let's go back to the studio, I have a manger who would like to meet you. He may be interested in buying some of my designs for his wife and I need you to model them for him." Like a fool, I went there with him. He gave me a couple more drinks to loosen me up of course. Before the manager arrived, he put on some sexy music. He stood in front of me and showed me how he wanted me to model the clothing. He said, "You have to be extremely erotic and sexy when modeling."

I kept repeating, "I'm scared," over and over. My resistance was met with more drinks being poured and shoved in my face. He poured more alcohol to get me in the mood.

Once the manager arrived, I felt tipsy. The fashion designer gave me the first outfit to put on. I complied and went to change. I came out and began to model for his manager friend. The fashion designer dimmed the lights and even put on a strobe light. Once the manager saw me, he reached in his pocket and began placing money all over my body. I felt confused. I thought I was just modeling. I overheard the manager tell the fashion designer, "Bring her to the club. I want her."

Once the manager left, I had a million questions for the fashion designer. "What was that? I thought I was only modeling clothes. Why was that guy giving me all this money?" At seventeen years old, his $200 seemed like a million dollars. "Just relax. I'll show you everything you need to know soon enough" He kept telling me to relax that he will show me soon. I ended up going home late that night. It was an extremely long commute.

The next morning, I felt weird. I vaguely remembered what had just happened the night before. I couldn't continue to think about it, so I pushed it to the back of my mind. I pretended like nothing happened. I went on with my day doing my normal routine. Now on my own, I still attempted to complete my high school diploma. I headed towards my high school internship for the day.

My internship placed me in a job where I worked in a courthouse. At the internship job, people noticed the changes in my attitude and behavior. It seemed I went from being a sweet innocent young lady to someone else overnight. People at work made comments, "Hey is everything okay with you," said one lawyer? "You seem rather tired a lot," said one clerk. "Hey, I noticed you're showing up late," said my immediate supervisor.

It was evident that I was not able to manage late nights and early mornings going to my internship. So I did my best to place more focus on completing my diploma and then working afterwards. While I tried to focus, the calls to dance did not stop. In fact, the calls increased. I was in high demand for modeling. Modeling as the fashion designer disguised and called it, slowly turned into full blown Exotic Dancing. The fashion designer kept up the façade for some time until eventually I was working full time inside of a Gentleman's Club.

No one seemed to care that I was underage. The club owners and bouncers looked the other way. All that seem to matter was that I was attractive and had sex appeal. Dancing in the club was not easy. I was extremely uncomfortable in that atmosphere. I faked it until I could make it. I forced myself to like it. I drank and smoked weed until I was floating around without a care in the world. The alcohol and drugs helped to put my mind in a place to continue dancing.

This went on for years. The fashion designer and I soon became more. He was the same person who introduced me to this lifestyle. All of this, while we carried on a relationship. He was almost forty years old. At home he was the boyfriend, but when we were at work it was something different. People would ask me if he was my pimp. I would always get defensive and say no, "I do not have no pimp." He would say that he was my manager so whatever I made he took a cut of the money. He did not care that I was out with other men. He didn't care because I was getting paid and bringing home money.

I worked in the clubs most days and every night while he was at work. After I graduated high school dancing became my full-time job. I started going into the club's early mornings, 11 am and staying all day into the night. I wouldn't leave until 1 or 2 in the morning most nights or stayed until closing at 4 am. Eventually I developed more comfortability with dancing and even had fun at times.

I became famous in the underground dance world. I was receiving calls daily and being booked for private parties every day. I had regular spots in different clubs. I began traveling in and out of state. I met people from all walks of life, this business was an escape for everyone. There were both men and women who came into the clubs, some professionals, like; lawyers, doctors, and even police officers. I had the pleasure of meeting several celebrities along the way. The celebrities were just like what you see in the movies. They look for the vixen girls or the groupies who are willing to do whatever. That wasn't my lane. I was very private and kept to myself. I was not the raunchy type of person. I never even called myself a stripper. Instead, I referred to myself as an exotic dancer. My innate shyness and elusiveness helped me reach upscale status. Upscale meant men paid to just be around me.

Before long I was averaging close to $1,000 on a good day, on a slow day I would leave with at least $300-$400. This was a huge business, clubs and underground spots all over the city, state and country. I had men paying my rent, car notes, bills etc. I was their trophy to carry around. Going out to dinners, concerts, wining and dining me on their dime. How could I say no? They wanted to be around a young female. I stroked their ego. There were plenty of older men who were willing to pay a bill just to be in my presence.

Everyone was looking for their fantasy to be fulfilled. Some people confided in me that they were stressed, and this was their form of relief. I became an expert in helping people get rid of their stresses by talking to them and making them feel special.

This lifestyle became very addicting. It's like when a person smokes for the first time, they do not automatically become addicted to smoking, they must continue until it becomes habit forming. The same thing applies with an alcoholic, they don't become drunk with the first drink, they must make themselves drunk time after time. Being able to make hundred and thousands of dollars, just being around people who paid for your attention. It felt like my needs were being met. I was receiving what I thought was love and attention from total strangers. I had some clients who specifically requested me. They followed me and kept up with my schedule.

I did not understand until later in my adult life, how I became every wife's terror. The truth was most men who were coming in this type of atmosphere were not single. They were married men. Many of them were willing to cheat on their wives. I learned to separate my emotions and become emotionless being in this environment. I was a sweetheart, but coldhearted at the same time. I had no morals; I did not care what people thought about me.

Navigating the dance world wasn't without its challenges. Many other females in the club were jealous and competitive. I sensed part of the dissention towards me came from the fact that I made money so easily. Many of the men in the club told me that I had a beautiful personality. They told me that they preferred more one on one conversation with me rather than dance. I could tell this made the other females angry. They had to work harder, spin around on the pole and do all sorts of tricks to get attention. I just had to be cute and conversate. Many of the females I was around and, in the clubs, openly expressed their jealousy during that time. I didn't care, I was just looking for love and trying to be happy.

Chapter 2
Professional by Day

More time passed. My boyfriend at that time set me up with a job. He talked me into becoming a volunteer in a municipal building where he worked to get my foot in the door. He worked there and did fashion designing on the side. I did what he told me and started volunteering there. I was scared and a bit nervous because most of the men who worked there had seen me perform in clubs and/or parties. Now I had to look them in the eyes and be professional which made me very uncomfortable. Many of them were worse than females. They could not wait to tell others who worked there, "she's a stripper," whispering behind my back. It was a challenge for me. I learned to ignore them and do my job. I was working in an environment, where I was surrounded by administrative professionals and troubled youth.

Ironically, I worked with troubled youth, but I was a troubled youth myself. It made the job somewhat easier; I especially could relate to the female population. Most of them were being detained because they had no place to go or were runaways. Some of them were dancing in the clubs, doing the same thing I was doing and living the same lifestyle. Who was I do judge them? I was still trying to find my way out as well. I suffered from the same issues they had. No real parental figures or guidance. Like them, my life was just all over the place. Here I was dancing for money at night, living with and in a relationship with a man who was twenty years my senior and just overall feeling lost. I just didn't know any better. That would soon change...

The volunteer position soon landed me a full-time job. It was quite a unique experience becoming hands-on with troubled youth. The pay was good, but I was still addicted to the nightlife. I would get off work and head straight to the club. I'd dance all night and wouldn't leave there until late into the morning, 4 or 5'am. I followed this by resting for a little bit before getting ready to start my day job shift in the morning. I would be so tired but the shift was busy so there was no time for sleep. It kept me on my toes.

This burning both ends of the candle stick continued for a period. It wasn't long before I was faced with another obstacle in my life. My younger sibling, who stayed with my aunt began reaching out to me more. It started with her wanting to spend more time together. She started hinting that she was uncomfortable in her environment. My aunt had been taking her to see a professional as if something were wrong with her. My sister was on psychotropic medication that made her angry, tired and gain weight. Finally, one day she came out and admitted that she was being molested by our aunt's boyfriend.

After we spoke about it, I told her that I was going to report the information she told me. My plan was to try to get custody of her so she could live with me. I pursued the matter. My supervisor warned me not to do it after I talked to him about it. At only twenty-three years old, he said, it was too much responsibility for me to take on. I didn't listen.

...ourt and was able to get custody of both my ... the courts ruled in my favor and ordered that my sister ... removed from my aunt's home. We showed evidence that my aunt had left them in the house by themselves, when they were underage which was against the law. Children's Services removed them from her home. They moved into my one-bedroom apartment. My boyfriend, the fashion designer had moved and gave me his apartment.

I managed caring for my siblings, teaching them the skills I learned from working with the youth at my job. I used what I learned at work and picked up what I was privy to learning from others. I enrolled them in good schools, attended parent teacher conferences and became a fulltime, twenty-three-year-old mother figure. I continued working fulltime, taking care of my siblings, managing salary as well as still juggling a few clubs or parties here and there for some extra cash. I was not happy about being on my own with my siblings without any help. So, I decided to move into the other apartment with my boyfriend. This was the Biggest Mistake of my life!

We were a busy house. My boyfriend was always out and about. He kept something going on with fashion shows while I worked and did the mother figure thing. Things were moving and we were all falling into the daily routine of life. Something was brewing under the surface that was set to rock my world.

My younger sister started maturing very fast. Her body started to develop. I didn't notice but my boyfriend began focusing a lot of attention on her. Then one night I had a dream that my boyfriend was going to try and molest her. I did not want to believe this dream or accept it. After I had this dream, wee hours in the morning, I immediately woke up out of my sleep to find this guy in the living room with my little sister at 3 am. I began yelling and screaming. "WHAT IS GOING ON HERE!!!! WHAT ARE YOU DOING WITH HER?!!! I was hype and livid asking him this. He sat silent, frozen. I turned to my sister, "You! Go to bed!!! I told her as he finally answered, "I was just talking to her giving her information." "At 3am in the morning," I glared at him in total disbelief. "I'm going to bed" we can talk about this in the morning he said. The next day I shared the dream I had with him. "Well if that's what you had a dream about then maybe you should move out." He said coldly, bluntly and matter of fact. What stood out to me was that he never confirmed nor denied it.

My boyfriend's niece often stayed with us and helped look out for my siblings. I was at the club working one early afternoon, and I received a message from my boyfriend's niece. She said, "You need to get home right away. There is something important I need to tell you." My breathing became shallow and I could feel my heart began to beat faster in my chest. It hit my spirit hard. I knew what she was going to say without her even saying it.

I went to my boss and asked to leave early. I was already on the phone calling a cab before the words left his lips that I could go. After I hung up the phone, I ordered an extra shot of alcohol. I stood outside and waiting for my ride. I was doing anything I could to calm myself. I felt worried, anxious, stressed out and confused at facing what I knew in my spirit was about to be revealed. I remember paying the taxi driver extra money to hurry up and drive the car now. I wasn't sure what to do or how I was going to handle the situation.

When I got home, I jumped out the cab after quickly paying the driver and rushed upstairs to the apartment. My sister was there seated on the couch with her head hung down. My boyfriend's niece was standing nearby in the kitchen with a look of disgust on her face. I looked from one to the other before bracing myself and sitting down on the couch next to my sister. She was quiet before she finally spoke. "He has been buying me a lot of sexy clothes and lingerie." She opened her hand to reveal the items that she had been holding balled up the whole time. "Did he have sex with you?" I asked her straight out. "No, it didn't get that far yet, but he has been trying, saying certain things. He molested me, fondling my body rubbing lotion on me and stuff. He has been asking me to do things that made me feel uncomfortable." This man really had a sickness, I thought to myself. After talking with my sister and hearing the whole story, I asked her, "Do you want to call or go to the police?" I paused waiting for her answer. "Or I could just kill him." I said with all seriousness. In the dream I saw myself stabbing him with a knife.

She said, "No let's just leave."

"Are you ok?" I asked.
"Yes, I'm ok."
"Are you mad," she asked?
"No honey. Not at you?" I couldn't believe she thought I was going to be mad at her.
"You know, you can talk to me about anything, Right?"
"I know," she said.

We packed up our things and moved out that night. We were fortunate that I never gave up the other apartment. My phone rang off the hook, nonstop. His niece must have shared it with other members of his family. Some of them called me hysterical. They were going crazy wondering if he was going to jail or not. Some of them were threatening to harm themselves if he did.

It was really difficult after that. I still had to work with this individual. I just pretended like I did not know him. I kept myself busy working at my job and doing my thing in the club occasionally. I was beyond hurt. How could this individual betray me like this? My focus became helping us all heal. I had to protect my family. I just let go and let God. It took a long time for us to heal from the situation. We got passed it but we never truly healed. I limited my contact with that person. I became bitter. I could no longer be around his family members at all. I was only comfortable with the niece that gave me the information.

All the while amid this chaos, I remember finding out that I was pregnant. My boyfriend's family suggested that I didn't have the baby; it was too much responsibility. I'm not proud of what I did in response or how I listened to them. Through it all God had a plan. I did not see what happened with my sister and this guy coming, but God did. God knows all things, even before they happen. God gave that to me in a dream, that my boyfriend would try and molest my sister. He was warning and preparing me. He stopped it from going all the way.

Chapter 3
My Life Flashes Before My Eyes

I met someone else while working on the job who helped take my mind off of everything. It seemed I was constantly attracted to older men now since the first guy. He was older but not as controlling. With the new man I was able to just have fun and live my life. Things were going great between us until I ended up getting pregnant.

I was excited to be a mom. Since I hadn't kept the first child I was looking forward to another chance at life. He threatened, "You better not have this baby…" Why can't I have this baby? I pleaded with him. "You better not or else." My excitement soon turned to sorrow. I was terrified not knowing what he would do to me if I proceeded with the pregnancy. He drove me to the abortion clinic. I was hurt, depressed because this was my second abortion. By the age of twenty-six. He drove me back home once the procedure was completed. I stopped speaking to him. He never checked on me to see if I was ok or anything.

I went back to work in the club like normal. I pretended as if I had lost the baby. I was roaming around and came across this man who had paid me for a dance. He was complaining about how his body was aching and I offered to give him a massage. He saw how strong my hands were. He said, "I'll pay you $300 for a full body massage." He booked a hotel and told me to meet him there. When I got there, I asked him to show me where I could freshen up. While in the bathroom, I called one of my girlfriends. I let her know that I was booked to do a massage and I would be done in an hour. We had plans to meet up later. I had ended my conversation with her on the phone and opened the door.

When I opened the door, I was staring down the barrel of a large gun in my face. My life flashed right before my eyes! I couldn't believe this man was holding a gun to my face.

"Oh my God!" I cried.
He said, "You know what this is, take it off". I had tons of jewelry on, so I thought he was robbing me for my jewelry. I slowly began to remove piece by piece.

He said, "No, B*!@#! Get on the bed! He began smacking me with the gun and yelling at me to perform oral sex on him. I felt a warm sensation flowing down my legs. I was so scared I urinated on myself.

I began calling out for God. I pleaded with God, asking Him, I said, "Lord if you can help me out of this situation, I would not go back to it again." I cried but inside I could feel my spirit began to rise. He put the gun in my mouth to keep me from making noise. He taunted me, "Where is your pimp? Is he outside the door, waiting for me?" When he removed the gun from my mouth, I begged him to please put a condom on. I made up a story stating I was expecting my cycle and I did not want to get any blood on him. Thank God, he listened, to me.

This man raped me and there was nothing I could do to stop him. As this man continuously raped me, he went through the entire pack of condoms. I pretended to enjoy. I figured it was better to play along to avoid him hurting me any further. That gun was so heavy, and it hurt every time he hit me with it. As he was down to the last condom he said, "Once I finish with these, I'm going to keep going all night."

I pleaded with him. I told him, "Please let me go. I have two daughters at home to return to. I must pick them up from the babysitter's house. They are expecting me soon. Please, I need to leave."

He told me, "Get dressed!" He held the gun on me as I did. He kept it by my side as he walked me to my car. He was going make sure that I did not do anything or alarm anyone to what had just happened. Once I got in my car, he immediately ran to his car and drove off.

I was in shock, but I had survived. The Holy Spirit who I had defiled for so many years, was right there to help me. I could feel and tell he had helped me get through the whole ordeal. He is the reason why I am still alive today and that man didn't take that gun and kill me.

I went back inside to tell the manager of the hotel what had took place. He looked at me with distained look and said, "I didn't see anyone." "But sir, there was a man who just beat and raped me." He picked up the phone and totally ignored me. I went home, got in the shower and cried all night. When I finally was able to talk to anyone, I told my girlfriend what happened and the owners of the club. They suggested that I go to the police. After the hotel manager didn't believe me, I decided against it. I was just happy to be alive.

Reflect: Can you think about a time your back was up against the wall, and you had no one to call on but the name of Jesus? Journal about the time you called on the name of Jesus, God, Our Heavenly Creator and he showed up and showed out to save you from what could have taken you out. Give thanks and praise, remember that God is always on time.

Chapter 4
The Vicious Cycle

This began to be a vicious cycle for me, of all these men and toxic relationships. I continued going from relationship to relationship and allowing men to walk all over me. I was too nice. During all these toxic relationships, attacks, abuse and negative encounters I slowly began to lose myself. I missed the "old me" who use to be strong, knew how to protect myself and didn't take any crap from any man. The "old me" would use them and leave them. Over time, I had softened up from wanting to be loved and just wanting affection. I wore my vulnerabilities like a badge and men could see them from a mile away.

Right before I ended the second pregnancy there was a private bachelor party, I did for one of my bookings. I met this wonderful man there who was mesmerized by me. We connected and exchanged numbers. Later after the incident with the attack at the hotel he reached out and we started dating. He became my end all be all. I fell in love so fast. We were inseparable or so it seemed. He was everything I ever wanted in a man. He spoke with authority and knew how to really treat a woman. He held a prestigious position with the government. Chivalry was his thing. He was the open the car door, pull out your chair, buy you dinner and roses kind of guy. I was so amazed and proud to be with him. He taught me how to cook almost everything. I felt so special every time I was around him. It was hard to believe that he was all mine. I felt as if I had to become a better person just for the relationship to survive. I made the decision to stop working in the clubs. I was content with just having my job and doing little side hustles here and there.

He taught me so much and I learned how to really care for a man being with him. In fact, to show my love for him I decided to get his name tattooed on my back. It was a painful and pleasurable experience at the same time. All it really did was stroke his ego. Something in our relationship changed. After that, he acted as if he owned me. I did not realize how vulnerable I become. Once I decided to show him my love for him, I became weak for him and had it bad.

Our fairy tale would soon hit a bump in the road. All the signs were there, and I ignored them all. He was always working late and not returning home. I refused to look at what was right in front of my face. I never question him about any of the signs, but just left things as they were.

Reflect: Did you ever ignore things during your relationship for the sake of continuing in the relationship? You knew deep inside that something was not right, but you continued to ignore it. Journal about the time you decided that it was not worth confronting what your gut was telling you.

_____
_____
_____
_____
_____
_____
_____
_____
_____
_____
_____
_____
_____
_____
_____

Chapter 5
A New Habit

I continued to the ignore the signs of my toxic relationship. I was too in love. We made plans to move out of state. I started applying for positions where we planned to move. My boyfriend had some connections and put in a good word for me at one of the state facilities in that area. I got a call back and they scheduled an interview.

Bad habits are hard to break. Drinking and smoking were still my regular thing. It's what I used back then to help me cope. I was used to being in the club having my drinks and smoking. This was the culture, nature of the clubs and the dancing life. Mostly everyone, especially the dancers drank and smoked. It's what we all did to be able to do the work we did. You had to get high to take your clothes off for strangers and money.

The clubs often got raided. They also had to pass inspections to maintain their liquor license. The smell from the smoke would be so strong that the club would get a fine every time police officers came to do an inspection or raid. Eventually they banned all of us from smoking inside the club. If any of us were caught, we would receive a fine or be kicked out.

The new rules caused the culture to suddenly switch. Everything changed. Girls started losing out on money because they could no longer get high in the club. A new culture and habit formed. Many dancers went from smoking to snorting.

I started seeing many of the girls fading away and losing weight. I had to know what diet they were on, totally oblivious. I was so naïve! I remember my mother always saying, whatever you do always keep your nose clean. I had no clue what she was talking about. I remember asking one my girlfriends, "Hey, you are looking slim, what kind of diet are you on?" She said, "Girl, you really want to know?" I said, "Yes, tell me because I need to lose some weight too." She reached in her bag and pulled out a small baggy containing some white powder in it. She said, "Try a little and see how you feel." I was scared and nervous but was desperate to lose a few pounds, so I did what was called a line. I remember feeling a drip go down my throat and thinking to myself, how does this make you feel good? It was nothing compared to smoking, but I went with the flow of things. I needed a new high and wanted to get slim.

I continued to get booked for private shows and parties. I noticed all around me that this was the norm. Everyone was snorting coke. The girls in the clubs, various parties and events seemed to all be going crazy over this stuff. Apparently so was I. It gave me a false sense of self. The illusion told lies to the user mind. It convinced me that I had more confidence and strength. It became the drug of choice for so many in the club because it was undetectable and did not have an odor.

I started seeing more dealers in the clubs. They pretended to be customers coming to get a dance. They really came because they knew their hot item would sell. A few of them tried to connect with me hoping I would bring them some other good clients. They told me they would give me a cut for every sale I referred.

I started bringing them people. I was getting a lot of clients to get the dealers candy. Some of them wanted to make sure that it was good stuff. They would have me to do a sample. I was their guinea pig. They looked to see if anything would happen to me. I wasn't all that comfortable or happy with this newfound venture, but I was very good with sales and persuasion. Never did I think about or imagine how caught up I was getting in this lifestyle.

To solidify my plans to move with my boyfriend, I found a job out of state. It was perfect for my boyfriend at the time and I to relocate. I drove out of state for the interview and drug testing. For some strange reason I convinced myself that If I drank all the detox formulas, I found in the GNC store that my system would be clear.

The lab called my phone. A woman's voice on the other end said, "Miss, there seems to be a problem. Your test came back positive for controlled substance. We need to know if you have had any procedures done or prescribed any medicine from a dentist." I was in total shock and denial.

The joke was on me and it was a very bad joke. All I could think about was the embarrassment I would cause my boyfriend. When we discussed our plans and I told him about the interview, he encouraged me. He said, "Don't worry baby you got this." I knew deep inside I was in trouble, but I did not know how to tell him. I knew I couldn't hide this from him. See, because my boyfriend was an official with the government. Not only did he refer me to the job, but he was familiar with the investigators I encountered.

He called me one day and was like, "Did you hear anything yet because I need to request a transfer. I'm not going to do anything until you get the green light. I know you will. "I told him what happened. I could tell by the way his voice changed that he was so disappointed in me.

He broke up with me. I tried to call him time after time and did not hear back from him until six months later. Our plans were ruined. I messed that all up shortly before I decided to give that lifestyle away, I was partying, hanging out with the girls and got caught up with some of the worst habits.

Chapter 6
Turning to God

I was so hurt when my boyfriend left me. I was depressed for several weeks. I remember being on the phone with one of the girls from the club and she said to me, open up a bible and read. God will fix your situation. It was hard to believe her at the time because we were getting high together, working in the clubs, so the last thing I wanted to hear about was how God was going to save someone like me. Yet, I listened because I had nothing else left in me. I had remaining candy left in my house at the time and I went straight to the bathroom with it and flushed it all down the toilet. I was not worried about losing out on any money. I wanted out, completely out.

Lord, Help me. That's what I pleaded. Please fix me, fix this. I don't know what to do it anymore. I felt so loved by this man and now he was gone. I tell you one thing about God. Be careful what you ask for. God Showed up and showed out. My girlfriend was begging me not to get rid of the candy and she would take a cab to my home and take it off of my hands, but I told her no, it's over. Instead of me selling all the dance clothing that I had that was worth thousands of dollars, I put it all in the garbage bag and threw it outside.

I gave my life to Christ. I became saved and filled with the Holy Spirit. I was a blood wash believer. No one could take me away from the love of Jesus. It's amazing how the same people that you do your dirt with is the same ones who can lead you out of trouble.

The devil was **BIG Mad**. It rained that night and when I got up in the morning, the garbage bag was completely opened and thrown on the ground. All of my clothing was all over the street, business cards with my name on them. I began crying, but I could hear the Lord saying to me, For His Name Sake I will have to suffer. Be not ashamed. So, I slowly started gathering all of my belongings that were spread out in the street and placed them back in the garbage.

I was completely sold out for Christ. I found a church home and was going consistently every week. I was even paying my tithes. I reached out to one of my aunts to let her know that I was on the straight and narrow path. She was so excited and proud of me. I joined her prayer group she had over the phone, and she introduced me to a spiritual world I knew nothing about. My aunt had explained to me that I would have to read this book called *"Pigs in the Parlor"* to understand what I was going to encounter. She and my grandmother were taking demonology classes at their church. They were knowledgeable about how and why people suffer with different types of addictions and diseases. They invited me to come over to their house and told me I would have to renounce everything bad or wrong in the sight of the Lord that I have ever done. This was like giving a confession to a High priest, I imagined. The only difference was that this was my bloodline and I was telling them everything I have ever done up until that time.

It was too intense for my grandmother. She was saying my God. She was shocked at the lifestyle I was living and what I had gone through. I trusted them because they were my family, so I went along with the process. They had prayed and fasted for this day and so did I. As I began renouncing things I began spitting up and throwing up and they were thanking and praising God. I had no clue as to what was going on, but I knew something was happening.

I was invited to another service that they had in the church and this time a man of God was conducting the teaching and service. This was on a higher level. I heard people screaming, crying, being physically aggressive. It was a lot. I remember the pastor calling out a telephone spirit and I felt something fly in my ear and I could not hear for about five or six seconds and then it flew out.

During the service I had my phone off. The moment I got back into the car I was anxious to let others know what I had gone through. My grandmother warned me not to get on the phone. She said you know you just got delivered from that you do not need anyone in your ear because that demon would come back. Now although I was saved, I was still stubborn. I wanted to do things my way. I turned my phone on and all you know what broke loose. Everyone was trying to call me, curse me out and get in my ear. I had to ignore the calls.

Living this new lifestyle was very challenging for me. I was different and it bothered people. They could not understand why I did not want them around me or in my ear. I stopped doing a lot of things that was considered of the world. I was completely sold out for God. I had set up an appointment to speak with the pastor of my church at the time to tell him about the deliverance I experienced.

I changed completely. Long gone was the dancing for money. I became a Mary Kay Consultant. I had put together a wonderful basket filled with Mary Kay items and I also added the demonology book. I never got a response from the pastor or first lady. I thought to myself, those products were expensive, and I paid my tithes. I was wondering if I was not doing enough.

Finally, the day came when I got to sit down in the office and speak with the man of God. He asked me, "What can I help you with young lady." I was so humbled and honored just to speak with him. I said, "Pastor, I had sent you and your wife a basket and there was a book inside…" I then told him my testimony on what I experienced being delivered.

The man of God then said to me, "Hear me and hear me well young lady. Don't you go promoting this nonsense in my church. You hear me? This is witchcraft." I did not know how to receive him. All I know is that I told the pastor what I had experienced, and he rejected my testimony. I wanted to cry but I held the tears in. I got up and went back to my seat in the pew and waited for the service to start. As I sat in the front pew, the pastor came out to the pulpit. He picked up the microphone and started preaching my testimony. He shouted at me with the microphone in his hand saying,

"Some of you are sitting right next to devils and witches. You do not need to see no exorcist to be delivered from a demon. We don't cast out demons we just call on the name of Jesus." He made fun of my testimony as I sat there, and tears rolling down my face. I turned over in my seat and got on my knees and began to pray. I needed to hear from God because I wanted to be obedient. I heard the Lord tell me, "Wipe the dust off your shoulders and don't go back." I could hear the pastor telling his security, "Watch her and carry her out if they have to."

After I left, some of the members who I was close to called me to ask what happened. I gave them my testimony and they were in shock. Some of them admitted that they too had struggles in certain areas but when they tried to tell the pastor he told them to just pray and they would get over it. They would pray but they were never truly free. After this experience I was so hurt that I did not trust going to any other church. I became bitter towards the word of God.

Reflect: Think about a time that you experienced church hurt. What changed your relationship with God? What turned you away from going to church? What created a disbelief in your heart? Journal about why you became angry with God, ask for forgiveness and forgive yourself.

_____

_____

_____

_____

_____

_____

_____

_____

_____

_____

_____

_____

_____

_____

Chapter 7
Backsliding

I received a phone call from my ex-boyfriend who had been gone for several months. He called me up as if nothing happened. I fell back into the trap; already hurt by the church I became a backslider. I started drinking again. I went back to other sins and fornicated with him. I was feeling all kinds of guilty.

Now that I was back with the love of my life everything seemed to be perfect. I met and started to bond with his children and family. I had a great relationship with his mom. There wasn't anything she could not ask of me. She became like a mother too me. Doing things for her was my way of giving back to my grandmother who was resting in heaven.

I was sitting in the car with someone that knew my boyfriend. I told them, "Guess what? I might be pregnant." their eyes flew wide open. Their next question and statement hit me right between the eyes. They asked me, "Are you stupid or what?" I stumbled on my words, "Why would you say that? I love him. He is everything to me. He is a wonderful man. We are building a life together…" Suddenly this person interrupted me and said, "He's married! You didn't know that?" My mouth almost hit the floor. Shock, hurt and anger were all understatements. I wanted to confront him so bad. I thought better of it. I knew his mom was sick at the time. We didn't know if she was going to make it or not. I held my peace. I played along like everything was fine. I did not say anything to him.

His mother got better, was released from the hospital and came back home. I stayed overnight at her house to help out. I was also waiting for him to come. He called his mother. I could hear him talking through the phone. The phone projected his voice. I heard him say, "Please don't let her touch my jacket. I left something inside." His mother was just nodding and shaking but I could hear everything he was talking to her about. I had to have answers. When his mother wasn't looking, I went straight to his jacket. I reached right inside his jacket pocket and pulled out a wedding band.

I was deeply hurt. I cried uncontrollably. I put the ring in my pocket. I kissed his mom and told her I had to leave and take care of some things. I acted as if nothing had happened. When I got home, he called me right away. "Have you seen anything or found anything important in my jacket?" "What are you talking about?" I denied it trying to see how far it would go or if he would finally confess or come clean. He kept digging for answers but never would admit that it was a ring or that he was married. Finally told him, "Yes, I have it. I found your wedding ring in your jacket pocket." He tried to make all kinds of excuses. "It doesn't belong to me," he said. "I really need it back though!" His voice changed and his tone became very demanding. He became defensive.

I asked myself, why was I was allowing this to happen. I just wanted to be loved by him. Now I learned that he was loving on someone else. He had a whole other life that I knew nothing about. My heart sunk in my chest. My thoughts raced and so much went through my mind. What was wrong with me? What did I do wrong? Why didn't he love me like I loved him? I thought to myself, "I must not be good enough."

My thoughts shifted to wonder, who was this woman he had married? What made her better or more worthy of love than me? I had to find out about her. I searched her out. I saw that she was highly educated. I learned what her credentials were. I decided to compete with her. I would go to school and obtain my degree. I thought that if I had a degree that he would want me and take me back. Surprisingly, I began working towards my Associates Degree in Applied Science. I was already working in the field so why not obtain my degree in this area, I thought. I settled for the A.A.S. I enrolled and attended John Jay College of Criminal Justice. I remember asking one of my family members if I should go for my bachelor's degree, but she said that she didn't think I would commit or finish a B.S. degree.

I fell back into my old sins with this guy. That's a place the enemy likes to keep us. The moment you do something wrong he will keep bringing things back to remembrance as if God will never forgive you. He wants you to stay stuck doing wrong and feeling bad. Sometimes we end up paying a price and live through the hurt and consequences of our sins. If you ever find yourself in this mental space, it's okay, we all fall short, just get back up. God loves us all. He hates sin but loves the sinner.

Reflect: Stop and ask yourself, what signs have I noticed? Did I discover that the person who I was in a relationship with or married to cheated? If so, what did you do? Did you stay in the relationship or marriage anyway? Write down your actions or thought process. Sometimes we choose not to confront the very situation that is hurting us. Do not ignore them, do not turn a blind eye because it can cost you a lot of hurt and pain.

_____

_____

_____

_____

_____

_____

_____

_____

_____

_____

_____

_____

_____

Journal about a time that you were so in love and you decided that no matter what you would put up with anything that came from that individual because you did not want to lose them or be alone.

Chapter 8
Self-Sabotage

This was my story. I loved this man with all my heart. I was under the illusion and delusion that we were going to get married one day. I was convinced that he only married another woman because of the hurt that I caused him. So, sadly I continued in the relationship with him. We stayed together on and off for a little over ten years.

I learned that he married and divorced at least two other women during our relationship. Not only had he married and divorced but he also fathered several other kids. It bothered me but I was hooked like a junkie on this man. It did not stop me from loving him. Right before his last marriage, he told me that he was ready for me to make him an honest man. I did not know whether to take him seriously.

We discussed the idea of relocating again so we could be together for good. He told me that he was ready for me. He told me to just hold out until he made some adjustments. He said that he knew that we were far away from each other. He said, he did not mind me dating in the meantime. He said he understood that I may need to get it out of my system so to speak.

I ate up his words. After all, I loved this man. I was so excited. everything was finally coming together as I wanted. I felt as if I waited all my life for this man. Nothing or no one would get in the way of us, or so I thought. I started getting messages from a man on Facebook. He told me he thought I was beautiful. He said he wanted to get to know me. I do not know why I went for this bait. I guess this was one of my weaknesses, I loved attention. This man was there, giving it all to me.

I had just finished reading the Steve Harvey book, "Straight Talk, No Chaser." I asked this man every question I read in that book. What was his long-term goals? What were his short-term goals? I asked him if he was ever married? I asked him if had any children. And, so on and so forth, one question after another. He shared that he just got out of a ten-year relationship. He said he was never married and that he had two children at the time. He satisfied all my questions. I obliged and we began seeing each other. I was physically attracted to him and thought that he was a decent man.

By now I was completely caught up in the world. One night while spending time with this man, my flesh took over me and we had a sexual encounter. He asked me if I was on birth control. "No," I told him was not at the time. We were both irresponsible and did not use protection.

I went to the pharmacy the next day. I picked up and took the morning after pill to avoid getting pregnant. It was too late. I was already pregnant. I started eating like crazy. I shared that information with him. He was in disbelief. "I don't believe you," he said. "It's true. I'm pregnant and its your child." I don't want anything to do with you or this child," was his response. I was completely devastated. It was hard to believe all the turns my life had taken. I was pregnant by a man I barely knew. Here I was pregnant, and the father of my child wanted no involvement during that time. I learned I was pregnant two weeks after my ex-boyfriend said he wanted us to get married. When he found out, he was devastated, I did it again. I hurt him in the worst way ever.

I didn't realize things would go the way they did but I knew that God is a Big God. I made a promise to God that if he ever blessed me with another child that I would keep the pregnancy no matter what. Like I mentioned before, be careful what you ask for. Ladies tell me why it is okay for a man to hurt us and women easily forgive them, but if we hurt a man, it's over and done with!

Reflect: Journal about the time your experienced this type of hurt.

Chapter 9
Life Continues

I continued with my college classes, pregnant and all. It was hard traveling back and forth to school during the hot summer. I managed and the professor was extremely accommodating. In the Summer of August 2011, I graduated with my associate degree in Applied Science in Criminal Justice, with a concentration on Conflict Resolution. I was proud of myself, but I felt like that was not enough. I did not attend my graduation because I was ashamed of my degree.

I was working overnight at my job, and overheard some co-workers talking. I remember the guy saying he was getting ready to graduate out of state, and in my mind, I was thinking how was that possible? So, I excused myself for eavesdropping and asked him to share more information with me. He told me he had taken online classes. He gave me a lot of information about starting classes online to complete my bachelor's degree.

I did my research and found Kaplan University online. They were an accredited school and seemed to have what I was looking for. I called them up right away. I ended up staying on the phone with the admissions department for two hours. Based off my recent degree, current career and experience they enrolled me in an advanced bachelor's degree program. I started in January of 2012. I worked and studied hard. I became an honor roll student. I completed my Bachelor of Science with a concentration on Juvenile Justice in January of 2013. I even graduated Cum Laude! I came a very long way! Go, me! It was the greatest feeling in the world. I traveled to Miami to celebrate my accomplishments with some friends.

Once I returned from my trip, I received a call from Kaplan University. The advisor congratulated me on my accomplishment. She offered me 20% off my tuition if I continued to my master's degree. I was nervous but with two degrees under my belt I was up for the task. I did not waste any time; I started the very next month in February of 2013. I graduated June of 2015 with my Master of Science, in Criminal Justice with a concentration on Leadership and Executive management.

I enjoyed taking classes online, learning new ways and ideas within my field. I received a promotion on my job and salary increase. A friend of mine asked me if I was going to go and get my Doctorate degree next. I told them do not dare me because I would do it. In the fall of 2015, I started working towards my PhD in Criminal Justice and Public Policy with Walden University.

This was a dream come true and an entirely different realm for me. There was no more babysitting and pleading with professors if you were going to be late with papers, etc. This was put your big girl undies on and get the job done. I even got to travel out of the country for one of my residencies. It was so amazing how when I got to Puerto Rico, the room was filled with African American and Latino Men and Women. I was confused for a moment. In my mind, people that looked like me was not willing to go that far to accomplish those achievements. I was wrong and it was quite the opposite.

We were all overachievers. We were not looking to prove anything more than we could do it. Between working fulltime, taking classes and traveling, I became overwhelmed. School had to take a back seat while I decided what my calling really was. I felt as if I was taking classes blindly just to be taking them. I began to question what was the urgency for the degree? I just felt I had to do it. Eventually, I took an extended leave from school. My plan was to resume no later than 2020. This gave me time to plan my work and work my plan.

Chapter 10
God's Plan, Not Mine

See, what most people think is that you go to school, graduate and then get a job, and that's all there is to life. Some are working strictly for benefits, and others and trying to make ends meet. I know that God has given me a purpose through all the pain and hardship I endured. I did not want to make my life so public, but that still voice is what kept me going. He wanted me to share my testimony to help save others who might have shared similar experiences. Today Human Trafficking is at an all time high globally. Young girls and grown women are being kidnapped into this lifestyle. I was never kidnapped. Admittedly this was a sound choice that was made. I made the choice, but it was through the power of manipulation. That's the message that I want both parents and young girls to understand.

We live in a world where sex, money and drugs are being portrayed as light or something good. Women are altering their bodies in hopes to be liked or loved by someone. I was there so I totally understand. It may seem so simple to those that are logical. Some are very analytical and try to make sense out of everything. But for those of us who have been impacted by traumatic upbringings and some form of abuse, none of what has happened to us makes logical sense.

I never felt loved as a child after I lost my grandparents. But what I have found is you have to learn how to love and appreciate yourself for who you are. Most women that I come across, in my peer group can identify with some of the things that I have gone through. The saddest part is most keep it all bottled up inside. For many of them, their silence has created bitterness, resentment, and made it extremely hard for them to love or trust anyone.

No matter what the pain is, you have to say to yourself, I forgive me, I forgive them, and put it all in God's hands. My advice is this…Do not allow the pain, hurt, worry and/or trauma to constantly remind you of what happened. Let go and move on! Write about it. Let others know so you can get the proper healing that you need. It took me 20 years to write about my life. I got tired of seeing so many women and young girls struggle with some of the very same issues I developed throughout my life.

If you never talked to anyone, and you do not feel comfortable talking about it. Journal! Write your most deep secrets and inner thoughts, so that you do not keep them bottled up inside. You do not want to become depressed, suicidal or better yet explosive anytime you are triggered behind something that reminds you of your trauma. Always remember that there is a root to any and everything. Where did the root start from? Did you allow that root to grow, did you attempt to cut it down? Think about it.

Reflect: How do you love yourself when you do not know what love is? How do you love yourself when you do not know how to love and receive love? Write about a time you felt that you did not love yourself and why? Write about the time, someone offered you love, and you rejected it because of any insecurities.

One of the challenges I had writing this book, was the after effect. What are people going to think, or say about me or my past? I had to come to grips that people are going to be who they are whether I write the book or not. They are going to talk regardless. I figured at least I could give them the information so they can get their stories straight. When you are in the hands of an abuser, abuse is abuse, point blank period! If you lie, cheat, steal, kill, rape, abuse, wrong is still wrong, it does not make one wrong better than the other. People always try to camouflage a lie with another lie. There is no such thing a pretty lie, or a white lie, is what I would tell some of the youth that I worked with.

There are so many people who protect abusers and get mad once they are exposed. You see it all over the media now, many celebrities, politicians, people of influence making headlines, for alleged abusive crimes that they have committed against young women and girls. Society is so conditioned that they are quick to talk down to and sabotage the victim who finally builds the courage to come forward. It does not matter how long it takes. You do not know what that individual may have endured all of their life behind any of these senseless acts. Common sense is not common for those who have been betrayed, manipulated by these abusers.

Who are we to judge, if what they are saying is factual or not if you are not the victim? It does not mean that they are being dishonest by waiting years or decades to come forward. That just means that they are finally fed up and do not want to see anyone suffer like they have suffered.

Some of the Red Flags and Signs for Parents To look Out for!

1. Any change in behavior, patterns, or routine.
2. Are they missing their curfew, skipping or failing classes?
3. How late are they on the phone? Talking or texting?
4. Are they requesting to spend the night over a friend's house? Is this often? Are you confirming with the parents? Make sure you know who the parents are? Most abusers are people we know and are familiar with!
5. Are they trying to dress or look older, than their age? Is the clothing too sexy? These are important key factors. You as the parent need to set the tone on how you want your daughter to carry herself.
6. Are you the parent working late hours all the time? Who is home with your daughter? Can they be trusted? We as parents need to be accountable as well in terms of the whereabouts of our children and the people, we entrust to watch over them.
7. Most importantly, do you have open communication with your children? Talk to them about respecting their bodies, and how they should not allow anyone to disrespect their temple and why! With everything going on in society today, children are way more advanced then we think. They are seeing sexual content on

television, so why not have a talk to explain do's and don'ts.
8. Are you checking out for signs to make sure that your child is not abusing drugs, you cannot smell everything? Teens and kids are more prone to swallow pills, and snort chemicals to get the high.
9. Make sure you consult with a health professional who can also check them out for any healthcare issues, such as drug abuse, or any sexually transmitted diseases, or infections. This is one way to know whether or not your child is active or abusing.
10. Don't expect anything that you are not implementing. If you the parent expect greatness from your child, you have to lead by example!

Note from the Author

I sincerely hope that everyone who has read this book was truly blessed by my testimony. It was not easy, but it was necessary. Mothers protect your daughters, Fathers be present in your daughter's life, let them know that they are truly loved by you. Do not take advantage of your authority and ever betray your daughter's trust by abusing her, but yet show her how she should be loved by showing that love and respect to her and her Mother.

Young ladies, if you have read this book and you are out in the world, you do not have to be of the world. You have the right to say no! Find out what your purpose is in life, create a list of things that you like to do. Pursue your purpose with passion, do not let anyone tell you that you can't do this or that. It takes time to build any foundation so know that with anything there will always be a process.

Try not to rush and do things in haste. Be patient and know who God is. You do not have to be perfect, just be you. Learn to love and appreciate you. The only validation you need is from yourself. It took me all my life to learn that.

Be Blessed, Inspired, and Encourage.

About the Author

Motivational Speaker, Coach & Published Author Adina Hodge is a very successful and accomplished CEO, Black Woman Professional and Entrepreneur. With several successful businesses to her credit, her entrepreneurial endeavors include a Radio Station, a Clothing Line, and Travel Agency. Her company, "She Helps Others Win" is where she launched her line of "She Helps Others Bling" complete with Blinged out T-Shirts & Accessories. In addition, she owns Exclusive Royalty Radio Station from which she launched and host her "Be Inspired" Radio Show.

She has a M.S in Criminal Justice, Leadership & Executive Management from Kaplan University and is a Doctoral Candidate for a PhD at Walden University. A single mother of one son, 7 year old Divine, she resides in the Bronx NY where she works as a supervisor for a youth juvenile detention center.

Support this Young Female Entrepreneurial Boss Mogul and her new book "VIP-Victim in Pursuit" by telling others and Following her on social media. Like her Adina Hodge page on Facebook.

Adina Hodge was a young girl who lost her innocence. Preyed on by a predator twice her age, she was lured into a life of sex, drugs, exotic dancing and prostitution. VIP is the heart felt, pounding, blood rushing, gripping tale of her story.

Adina says, I wrote this book once I reached the point where I said, "enough is enough". I had enough of watching young women like myself continue to fall victim to these older men predators and pedophiles. When I was lured into prostitution at only 17 an older man preyed on the fact that I was young and naive. He camouflaged his sex trafficking by calling it VIP. I decided to write this book VIP which stands for "Victim in Pursuit" to finally break my silence. Many may not understand the damage on the psyche of a child, who grows up without not having proper guidance, present, available or consistent parenting. This stunts the maturity and growth and keeps so many women in a vicious cycle even into adulthood. VIP is long overdue. VIP is here to set the captives free. Check out Adina's page to order any other copies.

Made in the USA
Columbia, SC
14 July 2022